William Taylor

Select Poems and Autobiography

William Taylor

Select Poems and Autobiography

ISBN/EAN: 9783337120078

Printed in Europe, USA, Canada, Australia, Japan

Cover: Foto ©ninafisch / pixelio.de

More available books at **www.hansebooks.com**

AND AUTOBIOGRAPHY

BY

WILLIAM TAYLOR.

ADAMS, INDIANA,
JAY C. SMITH, PRINTER.
1888.

Autobiography.

To the many friends who, time and again, have requested me to write and publish with my small collection of poems, an autobiography, I most respectfully subscribe such particulars as will serve, at least for outlines of a not very note-worthy pilgrimage. I feel assured that those who know me best, will exercise unlimited charity in order to smooth down many imperfections which doubtless will appear in this, my humble effort to place before them a few select poems, written not only in the dark, but under many other unfavorable circumstances, some of which I shall endeavor to make clear by the following briefly written testimony.

I was born of humble parentage, February 7, 1850, in Port Glasgow, Renfrewshire, Scotland. About five years later my parents removed to Whiteinch, a small village four miles west of Glasgow, where we resided eleven years. Just how much of this time was spent in school I do not know; nor can I remember much about my school days except a vivid recollection of a rattan exercise that a pedagogue executed most vigorously; your humble servant being the unfortunate recipient. In justice to the teacher I should note here that the severity was made manifold by a determination on my part to resent what I

believed to be undue punishment. My parents
sympathized with me, hence no force was used
to make me return to school. Thus, as it was
the only school in the neighborhood, my school
days were abruptly ended, when about eight
years of age.

Shortly after this my brother John, who was
about nineteen months my senior, engaged with
a dairyman to herd cattle. I agreed to help him
and so six months were spent pleasantly and
profitably. The following lines are in memory
of this pleasant time :

Do you ever think, my brother,
Of the time when you and I
Sported gaily with each other
By the Clyde when herding kye ?
And my brother, 'tis I know,
Five and twenty years ago.

We were happy then together,
Though too young for toilsome care ;
Yet in fair or foulest weather,
We were at our duty there,
Herding cattle, to and fro,
Five and twenty years ago.

Left in solitude, I ponder
O'er those days that 've long since fled :
And in thought I often wander,
O'er the paths we loved to tread,
Where the gowans used to grow,
Five and twenty years ago.

I recall with untold pleasure,
Many of our boyhood days,
When we rambled at our leisure,
Over Scotland's banks and braes,
Hunting bird nests high and low,
Five and twenty years ago.

But those days are gone, my brother,
Gone, alas, to come no more ;
Still I know we love each other,
As we did in days of yore.
When our young hearts were aglow,
Five and twenty years ago.

When the season was over, John got a place as grocer boy, and I with a boot and shoemaker to run errands. Here I remained, to the best of my knowledge, about eighteen months; next I was engaged with a tinsmith and gasfitter. About six months later he left for New Zealand and I was forced to find employment elsewhere, which I soon did in a shipyard,—boy's labor being greatly in demand at this time in heating rivets for iron built steamships. This I followed until about thirteen years of age, when I was bound for five years as an apprentice blacksmith to Barclay, Curl & Co., Whiteinch on the Clyde. A little more than three years elapsed when my father went to take charge of the blacksmith department in a large ship yard in Dublin, Ireland. My bond with Barclay, Curl & Co. was cancelled in order that I might go with him. We were in Dublin about ten months when John who was also a blacksmith thought to try his fortune in America. My father followed him one month later and we, my mother, sister, younger brother and myself returned to Scotland where we were to wait until my father could settle down. In about four months we learned that Cincinnati was to be our future home. While preparing to take our departure, an accident befell me July 4, 1867, While a

cousin was firing at a target, I stood near to see
where the bullet would strike. A piece of the
guncap penetrated the pupil of my left eye, caus-
ing great pain and loss of the sight. This de-
tained us until September 23, when we sailed
for New York, where my father met us at Cas-
tle Garden. Without delay we proceeded to
our destination arriving at Cincinnati two
days later. My father being soon dissatisfied
about the beginning of 1868 returned to his native land and the rest of the family removed to
Cochran, Indiana. Together we remained there
until October, 1871, when mother, sister and
younger brother returned to bonnie Scotland.
Meanwhile learning to love the land of my
adoption better than the land of my nativity, I
concluded to stay here.

I was at this time employed by Stedman
& Co., of Aurora, Indiana, where I subsequently
lost my sight. In the spring of 1872 I met for
the first time, Nellie Smith, the woman of my
choice. We united with the First Baptist
Church of Aurora and were baptized in the Ohio
river, February 23, 1873 by Rev. Chas. Ager,
pastor, who afterwards united us in marriage,
April 16, 1873. On March 22, 1874, Harold, our
first born came to bless our little home. But
the pleasure of seeing him to me was short. On
May 23 following, a sliver of steel from the head
of a tool I was using pierced the ball of my right
eye ushering me into lifelong darkness. And
were it not that my trust was in God, I scarcely
know how the calamity could have been borne.
But by the grace of God who doeth all things

for the best, I have learned to be satisfied ; and I fully expect when this pilgrimage is over to find that the so called calamity has been for some wise end.

Since my loss of sight, friends too numerous to mention have sprung up everywhere. I can truthfully say that I have never known what it is to be forsaken. Let me say in conclusion that my children, four of whom I have never seen, are all in all to me, while their mother is well worthy of the following lines :

Truest and purest of the human race,
From out whose breast compassion freely flows.
A being worthy of the highest place ;
And greatest blessing Heaven on man bestows.
True to her trust through dire, yet untold woes,
Though frail in form, still by her virtues strong,
Supporting man, beneath affliction's load
With holy love and sweet celestial song ;
And certes, in life's adamantine road.
True woman is the masterpiece of God.

Aurora, Ind., Nov. 5, 1888. WM. TAYLOR.

Poems.

Am I a Scot, or am I Not?

If I should bring a wagon o'er
From Scotland to Columbia's shore,
And by successive wear and tear,
The wagon soon should need repair;
Thus, when the tires are worn through,
Columbia's iron doth renew;
Likewise the fellies, hubs and spokes
Should be replaced by western oaks;
In course of time down goes the bed,
But here's one like it in its stead.
So bit by bit, in seven years,
All things are changed in bed and gears,
And still it seems as though it ought
To be the one from Scotland brought;
But when I think the matter o'er,
It ne'er was on a foreign shore,
And all that came across the sea,
Is only its identity.

I came a Scotchman, understand,
To live, by choice in this free land,
Wherein I've dwelt from day to day,
Till sixteen years have passed away.
If physiology be true,
My body has been changing too;
And though at first it did seem strange,
Yet science doth confirm the change;

And since I have the truth been taught
I wonder if I'm now a Scot?
Since all that came across the sea
Is only my identity.

My Native Land.

Oh! let me sing anither sang
 Ti' Scotia's rocky fells,
Whaur I hae sported aft amang
 The bonnie heather bells;
An' tho' I'm far across the sea
 Frae a' thy scenes sae grand,
I'll praise thee ti' the day I dee,
 My ain, my native land.

Tho' twenty years have passed away
 Since I bade thee adieu,
It seems as tho' 'twere yesterday
 I pu'd thy bells sae blue;
An' while's beside Ohio's stream
 In reverie I stand,
An' fancy it is a' a dream
 I've left my native land.

Tho' I, perchance, may climb nae mair
 Thy bonnie banks and braes,
Nor pu' thy flow'rs, sae fresh an' fair,
 As in my boyhood days,
Yet I shall tune anither lay,
 The best at my command,
In praise o' thee, tho' far away,
 My ain, my native land.

The Blind Man and His Boy.

The sky was clear, the air was calm,
The birds sang on the trees,
When I went rambling through the woods,
My children small to please;
The youngest two ran on before,
The eldest stayed with me,
When with a trembling voice he cried:
"I wish that you could see!"

"If you could see those lovely flow'rs
That cluster here and there,
And see those tall and stately trees,
That reach high in the air,
Then I might play with other boys,
And with them pleasures find,
But how could I enjoy their sports,
And know that you are blind?

"The trees are festooned all around,
With flow'rs of every hue,
The sun beams bright among their leaves,
Yet all is dark to you;
It makes me sad to see those birds,
So merry, blithe and free,
I often wish that we were dead,
Or else that you could see."

"You must not let such thoughts, my boy,
Disturb your youthful mind;
Remember, He who made those trees,
Has also made mankind;
And while He feeds the little birds,
That flit from tree to tree,

Will, if we put our trust in Him,
Take care of you and me.

"The sun whose rays in splendor shine
Among those leaves of green,
Shines ever on this world of ours,
Although not always seen ;
So do God's blessings ever flow
On them that walk aright ;
He has raised many friends to me
Since I have lost my sight.

"Then let us thank Him for His care,
And trust Him for His grace,
To guide us safely through this life,
And find our souls a place
Where neither grief nor sorrow comes
To mar the blessings given,
The blind may trust in God on earth
And see again in heaven.

A Boquet and a Wish.

A little lady gave to me
A lovely buttonhole boquet
And said she wished that I could see
The beauties of that sweet nosegay.

The fragrance should not be denied,
But ah ! thought I how little worth !
Too soon it must be tossed aside
To mingle with the mother earth.

Yet for the token of regard
My sincere thanks should be returned ;
And for the mind of some great bard
My very soul within me burned.

But all my humble muse would say
These flowers are very sweet I ween
While they must wither and decay
Your wish shall live an evergreen.

Home at Last.

The wand'ring minstrel has returned,
　　No more he needs to roam :
For his remains are safe inurned,
　　Whose song was, "Home, Sweet Home."

Without a spot to call his own,
　　He crossed the deep sea's foam,
And in a foreign land, alone,
　　He sang of "Home, Sweet Home."

He heard the maid of humble birth,
　　In music's sweetest strains,
Sing of the dearest place on earth—
　　That song was Howard Payne's.

And while the grandest martial bands
　　Enchanted royal ears
With "Home, Sweet Home" in foreign lands,
　　The homeless man shed tears.

At last, upon a stranger's bed,
　　Where he must cease to roam,
Kind angels came and gently said,
　　"John Howard Payne, come home."

The spirit of the bard took flight
　　Far o'er the highest dome,
And in the land where all is bright,
　　The singer found a home.

Though he who sang home's sweetest lay
　　Died on a distant shore,
And slept for years 'neath foreign clay,
　　He'll slumber there no more.

With honors spread on ev'ry hand,
  They brought him o'er the wave,
To find within his native land
  An honored poet's grave.

His wand'rings are forever past,
  No more he needs to roam ;
His resting-place is found at last—
  John Howard Payne is home.

Grant.

Arouse, ye minstrels, tune your lyres,
Ye, whose genius Heaven inspires,
Arise! and with your golden wires
  Chant high praise to U. S. Grant.

Tell the world what name is grander
Than Napoleon, the commander,
Greater far than Alexander;
  Praise the undefeated Grant.

Noble son of God's creation,
Whose great aim was preservation
Of the greatest, grandest nation,
  Ever graced the face of earth.

History records none specific,
Whose career was more prolific,
Nor can ancient hieroglyphic,
  Tell a greater name than Grant.

Glory shines in August splendor
Round the leader and defender.
Him, who rather than surrender,
  Would have died for liberty.

He has caused the world to wonder,
By his well directed thunder;
Bursting rebel ranks asunder
  And dissolving slavery's chains.

"On to Richmond," tells the story;
Battles won and fields so gory;
Lee's surrender seals the glory,
  Of eternal fame for Grant.

A Vagabond's Tale.

In years gone by, when in my youth,
  I saw and loved a flower,
And oh, thought I, it may forsooth
  Adorn some sacred bower;
And if it does, I'll neither tell
  Nor let my love be shown;
I'll bid the place a sad farewell,
  And go my way alone.
    Ah me! had I but known,

I found that it was not the pride
  Of any sacred bower,
And so, thought I, whate'er betide,
  I'll husband this sweet flower.
I thought of it by day and night,
  How priceless it had grown,
I praised its virtues with delight,
  And craved it for mine own.
    Ah me! had I but known.

With modest and with gentle grace
  That seemed almost divine,
Around my heart with fond embrace
  It lovingly did twine.

I guarded it with jealous care,
  And cherished it alone ;
No flower to me was half so fair
  As this I thought my own,
  Ah me! had I but known.

But ah, too soon, oh God above,
  The story's hard to tell,
The flower preferred another's love,
  And bade my home farewell.
He paused, a tear ran down his cheek,
  While one stole down my own ;
And when again he strove to speak,
  'Twas in a husky tone.
  Ah me! had I but known.

And now a vagabond I roam.
  With none to care for me,
No spot on earth to call my home,
  Although there used to be ;
And when at last my humble bier
  May be the earth alone,
A grave unhallowed by a tear,
  Unmarked by flower or stone.
  Ah me! had I but known.

But there's a home beyond the grave
  Where love can never die,
Prepared by him who died to save
  All sinners such as I ;
And there amidst that happy throng,
  Where sorrow is unknown,
I'll join the sweet celestial song
  Around the Master's throne.
  Ah me! I would be gone.

A Story.

"Mother, what makes your cheek so pale?"
A boy of twelve years cried,
"Have you received sad news by mail,
Telling some friend has died?
Or has it been some fault of mine?"
And as he speaks his arms entwine
Around his mother's neck,
"My mother dear, come tell me true,
What can it be that troubles you?
You are almost a wreck."

"Ah, no, my darling boy, my pride!
You have not grieved my breast;
Nor is it that some friend has died —
Not these disturb my rest.
And as the tears ran down her cheeks,
She kissed her boy and slowly speaks;
"'Tis for your father's sake,
He, who was once so true and brave,
Too soon must fill a drunkard's grave,
Oh God! my heart will break!

"Mother, where does my father go?"
The boy in anguish cried,
"For I can bring him home, I know,
Naught has he me denied;
We must not let this monster foe
Drag him down deep in endless woe,
The thought most drives me wild!
To bring him from the cursed den,
Of alcohol and drunken men,
God help a drunkard's child!"

The mother knelt in fervent prayer
To ask from heaven relief.
"Father," she said, "give us thy care
In this our time of grief.
But if it is thy will, O God !
That I should bear affliction's rod,
Then spare my darling child ;
And Father, if it be Thy will,
In kindness spare the imbecile
By alcohol beguiled.

"And thou, Great Potentate Divine,
Who made the earth and skies,
In pity hear this prayer of mine,
And do not me despise.
Do thou, O God. for thy Son's sake
Show my dear husband his mistake
And be to him a friend ;
Lead thou him from his evil ways,
And thou shalt have our hearty praise
Henceforth and without end."

The mother from her bended knees
Arose and dried her tears.
"My boy," she said, "my heart's at ease,
My mind is free from fear,
And if you will, my noble son,
You may down to the tavern run,
And take your father's hand,
And tell him, we would like him here
At home, his wife and child to cheer,
And make a happy band."

Emotion filled his youthful breast
At once with hope and fear.

"I'll go," he said, "at your request,
And bring my father here.
And mother, something seems to say
Our sorrows are to pass away
Ere many days are past."
But when they parted at the door,
They little thought they'd part no more ;
That parting was the last.

The lad straight to the tavern went,
And found his father there ;
He saw him o'er a table bent,
And heard him curse and swear.
The fiercest oaths were now and then
Indulged in by those drunken men,
Who wrangled in a game.
"Why does my father leave his home
To such a place as this to come?
Oh ! death before such shame !"

He stood and thought in sad despair,
Outside the bar-room door,
"If I should leave my father there,
My trouble would be more ;
For mother could not bear the grief,
And death alone would give relief;
Such loss I could not stand."
Then with a firm and manly stride,
The boy stood by his father's side.
And held his father's hand.

"Father," he whispered, "please come home,
The hour is turning late,
And mother longs for you to come,
Lamenting her sad fate.

Tonight she looks so very weak,
(And here the lad could scarcely speak)
I fear she nears her end ;
And father, neither you nor I
Can well afford to have her die,
Our dearest earthly friend.

The man though an inebriate,
Still loved his wife and son ;
"I'll go," said he, "ere it's too late,
This game may go undone."
Then throwing down the cards he had,
And rising to go with the lad,
He said, "I've drunk my last ;
Tonight my drinking days are o'er,
I here resolve to drink no more :
God help me to hold fast."

His drunken comrade from his chair,
Arose and cursing said :
"If that young boy were mine, I swear,
I'd lash him home to bed."
And as his hard and brawny hand
Came down with vengeance on the stand,
And as he madder grew,
Said he, "Joe Reynolds, you're to blame,
You have no right to quit the game,
Until the game is through."

Joe Reynolds angrily replied,
"I have no right to play,
But I've a right to quit," he cried,
"For aught Jim Jones may say ;
And if you do not like my plan,
Just do the very best you can,

Whatever that may be,
And I shall come and go at will,
A free man born, a free man still,
No man shall browbeat me."

Jim Jones, the man who kept the bar,
The hell-hole of the town,
Then raised a club he kept for war,
And struck Joe Reynolds down.
And Reynolds rising, siezed a glass,
And hurl'd it at Jim Jones.   Alas!
It struck the boy instead.
The lad fell lifeless on the floor,
A bleeding corse to rise no more.
The glass had cleav'd his head.

As Reynolds by the lamp-light's gleam
Beheld what he had done,
"O Christ!" he cried, "is this a dream?
Or did I slay my son?"
Then bending o'er the lifeless chil l,
He cried aloud in accents wild,
"Great Heavens! oh how sad!
There lies a mother's hope and joy!
Her heart was in her noble boy,
She'll die or else go mad!"

The father raised the lifeless form,
With heart so full of pain,
He did not hear the midnight storm
Of thunder and of rain.
His thoughts were of the boy that lay
A gory corpse, a lump of clay,
Whose life he did destroy.
He thought when at the garden gate,

Of them who oft for him did wait,
The mother and the boy.

Heart-rending were his sorrows now,
When in his cottage door,
He kissed the bleeding mangled brow,
And laid him on the floor.
The mother gazed toward her son,
One look and then her race was run,
Her sorrows, too, were passed.
The two who parted at the door,
In heaven had met to part more ;
That parting was the last.

"Maggie, my wife," Joe Reynolds cried,
In agonizing tones,
"I would to God that I had died,
Or else that vile Jim Jones.
It was at him I aimed the blow,
And not at our poor little Joe,
I'd die for him instead."
And when he stooped to kiss her brow,
He found that he was standing now,
In presence of the dead.

Go to yon bedlam o'er the hill ;
They've taken Reynolds there.
He wanders to and fro at will,
And cries in sad despair,
"Of alcohol when in the glass,
(A viper hidden in the grass)
A devilish snare, take care.
'Twas alcohol that drove me wild,
And made me kill my wife and child ;
Of alcohol, beware !"

Rest.

When I cast off this "mortal coil,"
And leave behind me care and toil,
Weep not for me, ('tis my request,)
But say a pilgrim's gone to rest;
When sorrow's blight no more can shed
It's baleful shadow o'er my head;
And thank for me the God who gave
The peaceful slumbers of the grave.

Afflicted, man has been from erst;
See how the newborn babe is cursed!
As sound vibrates within its ear,
How often does it start with fear!
And though unconscious of the cause
It writhes 'neath violated laws.
Thus from our birth pain seems to be
Fix'd in the human family.

Amid the gay and festive throng,
We join with laughter and with song,
When in our very depths of soul
Is anguish we can scarce control;
Perhaps for friendship we have lost,
Perhaps for friends by trouble toss'd,
Perhaps 'tis virtue basely sold
For filthy lucre, tempting gold.

For ev'ry flow'r along life's path,
Are countless thorns with pointed wrath;
E'en flow'rs of rich and rare perfume
Have pangs concealed amid their bloom;
Yea mortals breathe from purest air
The seeds of sickness and of care:

Nor need we hope life's ills to waive—
The only rest is in the grave.

Think not that they endowed with wealth
Can purchase happiness or health;
Think not the prince endow'd with pow'r
Can add unto his life an hour.
The master and the slave must trend
Their onward course to one great end;
Nor need we care when in the grave,
Which one was master, which was slave.

The monarch sits, scepter in hand,
And millions move at his command;
Yet with the peasant he is one—
A common life—one race to run;
Nor can his influence, his crown,
His royal robes, his wide renown,
Dispel the fears that rend his breast,
The grave alone can give him rest.

Our Lincoln's Hallow'd Tomb.

Oh haste thee, haste thee, verdant spring,
And grandest floral beauties bring
Of rich and rare perfume;
For Decoration Day draws near,
And there are those we should revere
Within the hallow'd tomb.

A nation that neglects the dead,
Who for its freedom freely bled,
Deserves not to be free.
Nor should a people e'er forget

They ne'er can liquidate the debt
They owe for liberty.

In memory of those who gave
Their lives our country's cause to save,
We would observe the day;
And though some lie in graves unknown,
Unmark'd by either flower or stone,
Their names shall live for aye.

The patriot whose race is run
Who rests with laurels truly won
Cares naught for tributes now.
Yet we, in homage to the brave,
May twine our garlands o'er his grave,
If not around his brow.

And thou, O God, help us to send
Our tributes from each state, to blend
In beauty and perfume.
And as the fragrance mingles free,
May all our hearts united be
To bless our Lincoln's tomb.

Memorial Day.

We gather here, Almighty God,
 In honor of our dead;
Some slumber here beneath the sod
 In their cold and silent bed,
And some lie sleeping far from here
 Beneath a southern sky,
Where none will shed a friendly tear,
 Nor mark the place they lie.

We give thee praise, Almighty God.
  That this our land is free ;
The slaves that once in bondage trod
  Are now at liberty.
And as the starry banners wave,
  Our breasts sincerely swell
For them who fought that flag to save,
  And for their country fell.

We bring these floral tributes here
  In token of our love
For friends who once were near and dear
  But now are gone above.
And as we strew the flowers around,
  We earnestly request
Thy blessings on each spot of ground
  Wherein our soldiers rest.

The Northern Lights. *

Hail ! to the lights that shone afar,
When our country was dark with blood and war,
Those lights that came with light'ning speed,
To serve their country in time of need :
And mid rebellion's smoke of war,
Each light lent its aid to the northern star ;
Whose glory shall forever shine.
In eternal fame on freedom's shrine.

Fathers whose beards were turning gray,
Call'd their stalwart sons on a bright spring day ;
My sons, they said, we must take heed,
Our home's in danger, our country's in need ;

*Dedicated to John A. Flatter Post, G. A. R.

Nor shall rebellion's legions dire,
Demolish our homes with their hellish fire;
While freedom's sons are hale as we,
The Union shall live and our land be free.

They volunteer'd with heart and hand
When the cry of war swept o'er the land;
They came on foot, and came on steed,
To serve their country, in the time of need;
Those gallant men must be admired,
Who rush'd to the front when Sumpter was fir'd,
And midst the southern shot and shell,
'Neath the stars and stripes for their country fell.

All hail! each patriotic band,
Whose glorious deeds shall forever stand;
Men, worthy of the name indeed,
Who served their country in the time of need;
And by whose valor tried and true,
Waves the stars and stripes in red, white and blue
Proclaiming far o'er land sea,
The Union still lives and our land is free.

The Preacher and His Man.

There was a preacher of some note,
Who owned a strip of land,
And as he could not work it all
He hired a helping hand.
The man he hired knew how to work,
So things went like a charm,
For while the preacher wrote his notes
The man toiled on the farm.

When Sunday came the man would go
To hear his master preach,

And listen with the utmost care
To what the text might teach.
Baptizing was the preacher's theme
And he took pains to say
That sprinkling is to Christ the Lord
As good as any way.

The man was of the Baptist faith,
And so was much surprised;
He knew the Scriptures plainly told
How Christ had been baptized;
He knew that down in Jordan's stream,
John did his Lord baptize,
So that the followers of Christ
Might go and do likewise.

The servant man desired to teach
The wise and learned man,
That to baptize is to immerse,
The Scriptures' only plan:
But how he might commence the task,
He studied all day long;
At length he settled on a plan,
Let it be right or wrong.

He took some seeds they had prepared
To plant down in the ground;
And spread them out upon the earth.
Then sprinkled dirt around.
The preacher came to view the work,
But could not understand;
He never had seen work like this,
So he call'd his hired hand.

"My friend," the preacher meekly said,
"There may be many ways,

But work like this, I never saw
In all my farming days.
If there is any law for this,
Explain it if you can,
To me there seems no sense at all,
In any such a plan."

"I took this plan I must confess,"
The working man replies,
"To teach you sprinkling is no way
For Christians to baptize.
I sprinkled those potatoes there
With dirt, to let you know,
We must obey the nat'ral law,
If we would have things grow,

"And when your work is ended here,
You need not be surprised
To find with all the sprinkling done,
You never have baptized.
Then follow in the paths of Christ,
As near as mortal can,
Baptizing in the good old way,
The Scriptures' only plan."

It is not I.

Lives there a man on this green earth,
  Of high, or low, or unknown birth,
Who sees the rose, so sweet and fair,
  And never craves the flower to wear?
If there be such in any land,
  His grave should be the desert sand,
Where not a flower may chance to bloom,
  Near by his undeserving tomb.

Cr is there one with heart so drear
  That music harshly grates his ear;
In whom emotion ne'er was stirred
  By cord, or reed, or minstrel bird?
If there is one, he should abide
  Far out upon the ocean wide,
And there beneath the briny wave,
  Find for himself a fitting grave.

Or one with soul so cold as this,
  Who never craved a lover's kiss,
But treads this pilgrimage of strife
  Without the purest balm of life?
Where should he go? I know not where—
  For earth unfit, unfit for air;
God only knows where he should dwell,
  And he won't say. Perhaps—Ah well.

To Chosen Friends Lodge, I. O. O. F.

Kind Brothers, in my humble way.
I wish to thank you all,
For this, another time your ears
Were open to my call.

I know that for my darksome lot,
Your sympathy still blends,
And I am glad my lot was cast
With such as "Chosen Friends."

Though clouds of darkness overhang
The path which I must tread,
Yet I can feel the cheerful rays,
That friends alone can shed.

And though Affliction's load is hard,
It partly makes amends,

For me to know my lot was cast,
With such as "Chosen Friends."

And brethren, I sincerely feel,
In this, my hour of need,
That you have been in truth and love,
A friend to me indeed.

So please accept the heartfelt thanks,
A grateful brother sends,
Who thanks his God his lot was cast
With such as "Chosen Friends."

A Blind Man's Visit.

I went to chat with the Foundry Boys,
   And as the day was fine,
I spent it well amid the noise
   For the days of Auld Lang Syne.

The pleasure that it gave to me,
   I cannot well define,
Although the boys I could not see
   As in days of Auld Lang Syne.

Their hands I took and warmly shook,
   As warmly they did mine,
And hearty were the laughs we took
   At the days of Auld Lang Syne.

While standing near the blacksmith fire
   That once was known as mine,
There came to me a strong desire
   For the days of Auld Lang Syne.

Though I should live for many years,
   E'en ninety years and nine,
My eyes would fill with joyful tears
   For the days of Auld Lang Syne.

A Type of Man.

One morning in the summer time,
When nature truly was sublime—
  Not e'en a cloud was seen—
Up o'er the hills I bent my way
To spend a quiet holiday
  Among the living green ;
And while beside a mountain brook,
Within a cool sequestered nook
I sat and watched with eager look
  The water as it ran,
I thought I saw in nature's book
  A perfect type of man.

The stream ran downward in its course,
And I arose to find its source—
  I might say place of birth ;
And near the summit of a hill
I saw a little running rill
  Spring from the mother earth.
It crept along a narrow bed—
I followed on where'er it led,
And saw it as it onward sped
  Grow stronger as it ran.
How like (unto myself I said)
  The infancy of man.

In innocence it went its way
As doth a child in childish play,
  Nor bent on good nor ill ;
It leap'd and sprang, it seem'd to me
Just like a child in childish glee
  When left to sport at will ;

And yet anon a shadow fell—
An omen seeming to foretell
That e'en a flower may cast a spell
   Of darkness o'er our face.
'Tis thus, thought I, fate doth dispel
   Some sunshine of our race.

From either side the brook was fed
By streams fine as a silken thread,
   And pearly drops of dew;
While bending o'er in rural bliss,
With benediction and a kiss,
   Were flowers of every hue.
These lent enchantment to the scene,
And yet the brook with boyish mien
Rushed onward to a dark ravine.
   So (thought I) as it ran,
On earth there never yet hath been
   A truer type of man.

Now like a thoughtless aimless youth,
With face alternate rough and smooth,
   It hurried cheerily,
Unmindful of the hidden wrath
That lay awaiting in its path.
   On to its destiny.
The wayside fountains joined to swell
Its volume as adown the dell
O'er rock and precipice it fell;
   The spray seem'd like our tears
When we are bidding a farewell
   To scenes of childhood years.

But ere it reached the mountain base
It moved with stately, manlike grace,
   As if 'twas tired of play,

And that employment it must find,
And be of use to all mankind
  Ere it should pass away.
Its idleness was near an end,
As to a lake it did descend,
And there with other streams did blend
  In perfect harmony :
Then from the lake they slowly wend
  Their way in company.

I follow'd on around a hill,
And soon I saw a paper mill
  Run by this swollen stream,
Whence leaves for books of every kind
That now expand the human mind,
  And wing the poet's dream.
A flax, then cotton mill appear'd,
Which enterprising man had rear'd,
And so until the end was near'd
  Its labor was applied.
The stream I silently revered
  With bared head by its side.

Now like a sage whose life was spent
In usefulness, it seem'd content
  To calmly fall asleep.
With strength subdued and furrow'd face,
It now had run its destined race,
  And mingled with the deep.
'Tis thus, thought I, with all mankind ;
From youth to age we are inclined
To seek the path for us design'd,
  And serve in some great plan :
The brook is clearly in my mind,
  A perfect type of man.

To a Friend.

Respected and much valued friend,
To you these humble lines are pen'd ;
An' whaur th' muse is gaun tae end
    I dinna ken ; but on this fac' ye may depend,
      I'll haud th' pen.

It daes a Scotchman guid, ye ken,
Tae meet anither noo an' then,
An' crack o' Scotia's things an' men,
    When far awa
Fra ilka Scottish hill and glen,
    An' birken shaw.

When Scot meets Scot they like tae speir
Aboot auld haunts that still are dear ;
An' braid Scotch tongues they like tae hear
    Whan o'er the sea ;
For Scotland, Scotchman will revere
    Untae th' dee.

There's something in a guid auld sang,
Sung in the braidest Scottish twang,
That gaurs Scotch bluid tae loup alang
    Wi' dooble speed ;
An' tho' th' tune be richt or wrang,
    They dinna heed.

Tho' Caledonians haud wi' pride
Columbia as their chosen bride,
They ne'er forget th' auld fireside—
    Th' mither hame.
An' if their love they sude divide,
    Wha wad them blame?

Then chide us not, if we by spells
Look back wi' pride on Scotland's fells,
Whaur grew the bonny heather bells
   Amaist divine;
An' gowan'd braes an flow'ry dells
   O' auld lang syne.

A Tear for Caledonia.

Though far from Scotia's rugged hills,
  Her birken shaws and dells,
And though I never more may cull
  The bonnie heather bells,
Still I shall love her broomie knowes,
  Her fountains bright and clear,
And for the days of "Auld Lang Syne"
  I sometimes shed a tear.

While I admire Columbia's shore,
  The great land of the free,
Whose broad majestic rivers roll
  In grandeur to the sea;
And though I've met with many friends
  Who now to me are dear,
Yet for the land that gave me birth
  I sometimes shed a tear.

I hear some praise the sunny south,
  Where sweet magnolias bloom,
And where the orange blossom sheds
  Abroad its sweet perfume;
And where the feather'd warblers' songs
  Enchant the list'ning ear;
Yet for the land of Robert Burns
  I sometimes shed a tear.

The minstrel may forego his harp,
  The bird may leave its nest,
The mother may forsake the child
  She's nourish'd at her breast;
But Scotland I shall ne'er forget
  To honor and revere.
And for the land I'll see no more
  I'll wipe away a tear.

Who is it?

Within Aurora there does dwell
A man whose surname I shall spell,
A word shall give the proper sound
To ev'ry letter therein found,
And if these lines you closely scan
You may at once discern my man;
I shall begin on number nine,
Then one on each alternate line.
It happened when I used to BE
Within a land far o'er the sea
Where there ARE flow'rs o'er hill and dell
And pride of all the heather bell,
But Oh! I saw a lovely flow'r
Within a rural cottage bower,
Near by the flow'ry banks of DEE,
She was the fairest flower to me
And were I but a honey BEE
From her sweet lips I ne'er would flee,
Her E'E was black as any sloe
And haunts me now where'er I go;
A finer form you ne'er would SEE
On any Scottish hill or lea,

A bonny lass was Ellen K
As all the lads were wont to say.
So now that I have spell'd his name
It rests with you to find the same.

A Diamond.

Oh!
Never
Dissever
The holy ties
Nor do thou despise
The bonds that bind thy soul
To heaven's eternal goal;
Where Christ our king shall reign for aye :
Rather with a contrite spirit pray
For Him to take thy sins away.
Thus the faith that binds thy soul
To that eternal goal
Will not be shaken,
Nor forsaken,
But nearer,
Dearer
Grow.

"Whig."

The following lines were written in answer to a friend who desired to know how and where the word "Whig" originated. The first word in each verse make up the motto, "We Hope In God"

'We Hope in God," an ensign bore
In Scotland years ago ;
Supported by a broad claymore,
It fluttered to and fro;

And after a great battle won
  The flag still floated free,
But of the letters there were none,
  Save W—H—I—G.

Hope ran through each and every breast
  Like wild waves o'er a main :
Each felt that he had done his best,
  And would do so again.
And when they saw their flag bereft
  Of parts they loved to see,
They thanked their God that still were left
  The W—H—I—G.

In God they placed implicit trust
  That all would yet be right ;
Full well they knew their cause was just,
  Which gave their valor might.
The flag by Scottish knights sustained,
  Now waved o'er hill and lea,
And all the motto it contained
  Was W—H—I—G.

God sped the cause o'er hill and dale,
  To hut and lordly hall ;
The lowly Scot and sturdy Gael
  No tyrant should enthrall.
And so it sped across the seas,
  Where all men now are free,
And flung its banner to the breeze
  With W—H—I—G.

Tubal Cain the Founder.

I sing about a genius grand,
  Whose name and fame is sure to stand

As good as any in the land,
  His name is Tubal Cain.

'Twas he who first the iron found
And brought it from the miry ground ;
With echoes let the welkin sound
  In praise of Tubal Cain.

The chisel in the mason's hand
That hews the rocks for lighthouse grand
To warn the sailors off the strand,
  Is due to Tubal Cain.

The stuff that makes the iron steed,
That travels on with lightning speed,
O'er mountain rough or level mead,
  Was found by Tubal Cain.

The wires that gird around the earth
To carry news of woe or mirth,
Or tell of marriage, death or birth,
  We owe to Tubal Cain.

The bell that hangs neath yonder spire
And tolls for infant, youth and sire,
Or clamors out with news of fire
  Is due to Tubal Cain.

The cannon ball and monster gun
That made proud Johnny Bull to run,
The nicest job beneath the sun,
  We owe to Tubal Cain.

Then send your praises o'er the land
In honor of this genius grand,
And when you grasp a brother's hand,
  Just mention Tubal Cain.

To William Taylor Dowrey and Wife on the Death of their Son, Scotty.

Within the eden of your hearts
   There came a lovely vine,
Whose tender shoots with loving clasp
   Around your hearts did twine,
And with a parent's fondest love
   Your tender cares were given
To him whose happy face appeared
   A blessing sent from heaven.

Beneath the cutting wintry blast,
   That comes to one and all,
The vine that promised splendid fruit,
   Too soon, alas, must fall.
And from the dearest earthly ties
   Wee Scotty has been riven
And wafted to the better land
   To bloom with Christ in Heaven.

The great Creator's wondrous ways
   Are hard to understand—
The upright and the trusting ones
   Oft feel the chastening hand.
But let us hope that we shall find
   Our trials have been given
To lead us from our earthly way
   And turn our thoughts to Heaven.

Charity.

Chide not in haste the erring man,
Before you censure, calmly halt
And give yourself a thorough scan,
And see if you have not one fault.

Since Adam in the garden fell,
To err has been our earthly doom;
And there is none that doeth well,
The faultless live beyond the tomb.

Extend your charity, O man,
Unto the frail misguided one;
The poor forlorn, with face so wan,
May have a destined race to run.
The great may not be always great,
Nor may the wise be always wise;
And why should we not deviate
When angels fell from Paradise?

Do not contemn the feeble man,
Look not on such with cruel scorn;
Perhaps he does the best he can,
It may be weakness with him born.
And though unequal in our eyes,
He is no less a brother still;
Then oh ye great, ye good, ye wise,
Be gentle to the imbecile.

Civility.

We mortals ne'er should disagree,
  For we are truly brothers;
The members of one family,
  Though born of many mothers.
To live in unity is best,
  Dissension doth bring evil;
And if on earth we would be blest,
  We must be justly civil.

Let politicians all agree
  To quit their wrangling chorus;

What signifies to you or me
  What people did before us?
And let the lawyer cease to twist
  The law round like a swivel;
Let peace and harmony exist—
  Be civil, men, be civil.

Let us remember Christ's command—
  'Tis "Love ye one another,"
And ever reach a helping hand
  To aid a fallen brother—.
For man's injustice unto man
  Sends thousands to the devil,
When it is much a better plan
  To be both just and civil.

And we should ever bear in mind,
  As down life's stream we're gliding;
That it is better to be kind,
  Than be forever chiding.
For though we live threescore and ten,
  We have no time to cavil;
Then let us try, as honest men,
  To be upright and civil.

The Artisan.

Be not by vanity mis-led
  To slight the artisan,
For though he toils to earn his bread,
  He's nature's nobleman:
Yea, quite as worthy as a king
Is he who makes the anvil ring,
And from whose brow flow streams of sweat,
To pay the law of nature's debt.

The monuments of Art go view,
    By men of genius wrought,
Nor grudge the workman honor due
    Though humble be his lot.
The prince may come in grand parade,
But soon such pageant glories fade,
While through all ages shall remain
The name and fame of Tubal-Cain.

The stately vessel reared by skill
    Ploughs through the deep blue main,
The steam steed climbs the rugged hill
    And speeds across the plain,
E'en lightning comes as by command
To carry news from land to land,
And now the grand electric light
Makes bright as day the darkest night.

Among the nations of the earth
    The works of Art abound,
Nor can we estimate their worth
    Wherever they are found.
Then look not on the genius Lorn
With cold contempt, or cruel scorn,
Though poor, the honest artisan
Has earned the title—Nobleman.

The Poet.

The poet's path is very hard,
    And countless ills his fate,
Yet he who'd gain a bard's reward,
    Must never deviate ;
And with a firm, determined stride
Move onward up the mountain side.

The mountain path that leads to fame,
   Is ever steep and rough,
And he who climbs must not be lame,
   He'll find this soon enough ;
For critics with keen weapons stand
To hew him down on every hand.

Amid the scorpion critic's jeers,
   He firmly wends his way ;
And when their scoffs are turned to cheers,
   He has no time to stay ;
The summit is his only aim
Whereby to earn a poet's name.

When hemm'd by want of learning great,
   The bard appears forlorn,
And now and then, it seems that fate
   Would crush the poet born ;
But with Pegasus at his call,
He mounts his steed and needs not fall.

O'er barriers of untold height,
   And ravines deep and wide,
He fearless rides with true delight,
   To venture is his pride;
Nor thinks he once from whence he came,
His only aim, a poet's fame.

To Whom It May Concern.

This poem was written upon receiving an April Fool package with thirty nine cents arrears for postage.

Oh! for Lord Byron's fiery tongue,
And pen of Walter Scott
To scourge the meanest rogue unhung,
Who thinks I know him not.

He thinks because he takes it cool
And ignorant appears,
That I don't know he sent that fool
With thirty-nine arrears.

I know him well, his writing's known,
The low scurrillous whelp!
Nor do I think he was alone—
Of course he had some help.

Some mail official must have lent
His service to the scamp;
The envelope was marked "missent,"
And had a bogus stamp.

I wish that he had taken thought
And sent his autograph,
For I sincerely think it ought
To head this epitaph:

"Here lies a caitiff and foul reprobate
Whose tooth was venom and whose soul was hate
Conniving wretch whose loathesome breath did
He was a reptile of the haunts of hell;   [tell
A dastard scoundrel of the deepest dye,
Whose ignominious actions verify,
For none but such would stoop so low to find
A scheme to trap the unsuspecting blind."

But if he deems this not enough,
Then let him make it known,
And with a budget of such stuff
I'll cheerfully atone.

The Sailor Boy's Grave.

The sun disappeared o'er a calm blue sea
  At the close of a summer day,

And the sea gulls were resting quietly,
  On the breast of a silent bay ;
While a bark lay waiting a friendly breeze
  To waft it away to its native seas.

But midnight beheld a terrific storm—
  How the winds and the waves did roar !
And the lightning's flash showed the bark's
      frail form
  To watchmen patroling the shore ;
And they knew that no mortal hand could save
  That fated bark from a watery g ave.

On the following morn at early dawn,
  When the hurricane's work was done,
Came a drifting spar with a boy lash'd on,
  But his earthly career was run ;
And the children wept for the boy in blue,
  Who was drown'd that night and whom no
      one knew.

They laid him to rest in the church yard green
  Near a spot where the woodbine grew,
And they raised a slab where it might be seen
  To remember the boy in blue.
And the children go to the rippling wave
  To gather sea shells for the unknown's grave.

At twilight I stood where the sea boy lies,
  And thought, if on some distant shore,
A mother is watching with tearful eyes,
  For her boy who'll return no more,
An angel might whisper, far o'er the wave
  Strange children with shells deck your dar-
      ling's grave.

The Gowans and Blue Bells.

There are flowers o'er the sea,
That will aye be dear to me,
Though there may be flowers in other lands
But the gowans and blue bells   [more rare;
On fair Scotland's hills and dells,
Are the bonniest and the sweetest I declare.

CHORUS.

Oh the gowans and the blue bells
On fair Scotland's hills and dells,
Are the sweetest flowers that ever decked a lea;
But I'll see them never more,
On fair Scotland's lovely shore,
For I'm doomed to wander far across the sea.

Let the jessamine so rare
Be the Indian's boast and care,
And let others praise the lily of the vale;
But my bosom proudly swells
For the gowans and blue bells   [dale.
That are found on bonnie Scotland's hill and

In my dreams I often roam
To my happy childhood's home,
Where the gowans shine like diamonds on the lea;
And my heart will yearn in vain
For my native land again,
When I wake to find I'm far across the sea.

But as I must wander wide,
Frae the bonnie river Clyde,
Where I've sported in my youth along the
I am forced to say farewell   [shore;
To the gowan and blue bell,
For I'll never, never see them any more.

Reason.

If Voltaire, Spencer. Huxley, Darwin or Laplace
Perchance had been the offspring of some Lea-
    then race,
With naught but heathen influence, should we
    expect
That either would have had such mighty intel-
    lect.

But if it is in Christian lands alone we find
One like Voltaire, with such superb, colossal
    mind,
Then would it be unjust for us to boldly say
His eminence is due to Christianity?

The atheistic evolutionist in pride
Thus stultifies himself that God may be denied.
And vainly tries to teach his dogma to the world :
That Christianity should from the earth be
    hurl'd.

He who would sweep the Christian doctrine off
    the earth
Would banish that which gives immortal great-
    ness birth ;
And he who should to such ignoble actions bend
Unmanly turns in wrath against his greatest
    friend.

Wayside Thoughts.

Fickle friends are like reflections,
  On life's sea when bright and still ;
Then you'll find in all directions,
  They do follow at your will ;

But let darkness overtake you,
And destructive billows roar,
Then your fickle friends forsake you,
Though life's bark be cast ashore.

He who would to the summit rise
Must not the shortest step despise;
And if a step you cannot gain,
Turn not from half one in disdain;
The road to fame is rough and steep,
And he who climbs must often creep.
The timber of the greatest worth,
Is that which has the slowest growth;
A mush-room springs up in a night
Another and 'tis out of sight.

The more we see and understand,
The works of the Creator's hand,
The more we feel ourselves to be
Dependent on His charity.

There seems to be a sense innate,
Whereby an intellectual mind
May faithfully discriminate,
With whom we should associate;
And thus it is we often find
That instant love, or instant hate,
Remains forever undefined.

The Aurora Gondolier.

Yes! richer by far
Than lute or guitar
Or harp of a thousand strings,

Are the notes so clear,
Of the gondolier,
As he rows his boat and sings.

"How I love to row
On the Ohio —
When she that I love is near,
On a summer night
When the stars are bright,
And the moon is shining clear."

With heart all aglow,
To Split Rock he'll row,
To join a picnic on shore,
And his joyous song,
As he rows along,
Keeps time with the dipping oar.

The echoes rebound
From the hills around,
Enchanting the l'st'ning ear,
While proud as a king,
He'll merrily sing
The song of the gondolier.

"How I love to row
On the Ohio—
When she that I love is near,
On a summer night
When the stars are bright,
And the moon is shining clear."

To the Memory of the Poet,
H. W. Longfellow.

In mountain homes and city halls,
Longfellow's songs are sung ;
They've found the way to foreign lands,
And to the foreign tongue.
They give Columbia's bard a name,
Throughout his native land;
And fame that will not fade away,
Like foot-prints on the sand.

There may be bards in other lands,
With more romantic style ;
But none whose themes are more sincere
Nor thoughts more free from guile.
For more than threescore years and ten,
An upright life he led ;
But he who wrote Evangeline,
Now slumbers with the dead.

How beautiful the Psalm of Life
Portrays his noble mind ;
The Village Smith and Haunted Slave
Endears him to mankind.
Excelsior, the Clock, and Bridge
Shall stand forever more,
To bless the poet, born to fame.
On fair Columbia's shore.

And now the Angel of the Lord,
Whose voice all must obey,
Has come, his mission to fulfill,
Our bard to take away.
Away from all those worldly cares,
That oft did fill his breast ;
Our loss is his eternal gain.;
Longfellow is at rest.

www.ingramcontent.com/pod-product-compliance
Lightning Source LLC
Chambersburg PA
CBHW022041080426
42733CB00007B/934